These pearls of thought in Persian gulf were bred,
Each softly lucent as a rounded moon;
The diver Omar plucked them from their bed,
Fitzgerald strung them on an English thread.

Lowell

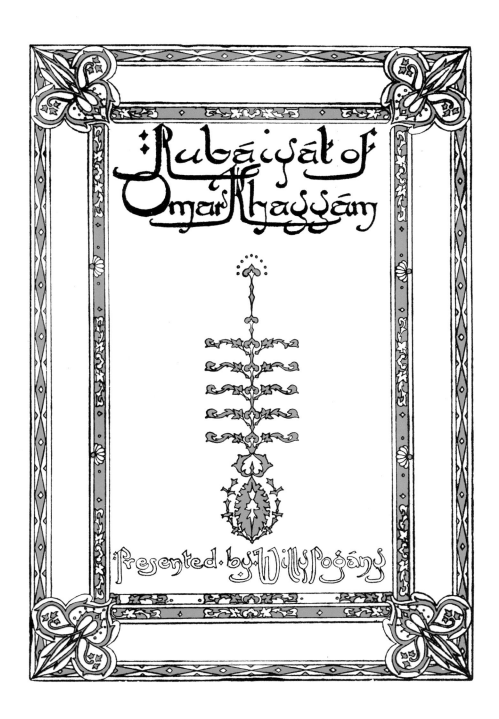

Rubáiyát of Omar Khayyám

Presented by Willy Pogány

BLOOMSBURY BOOKS
LONDON

First edition published in Great Britain 1984
by HARRAP LIMITED

19–23 Ludgate Hill, London EC4M 7PD

Reprinted: 1984; 1985

This edition published 1988 by
Bloomsbury Books an imprint of
Godfrey Cave Associates Limited
42 Bloomsbury Street, London WC1B 3QJ

ISBN 1 870630 65 3

Printed in Yugoslavia

1

Awake! for Morning in the
    Bowl of Night
Has flung the Stone that puts
    the Stars to Flight:
And lo! the Hunter of
    the East has caught
The Sultán's Turret in a
    Noose of Light.

II

reaming when Dawn's Left
    Hand was in the Sky,
I heard a Voice within the
    Tavern cry,
"Awake, my Little ones,
    and fill the Cup
Before Life's Liquor in its
    Cup be dry."

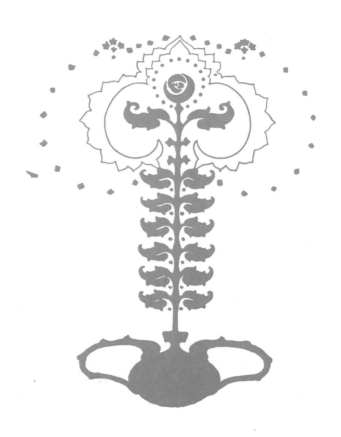

III

nd as the Cock crew, those
who stood before
The Tavern shouted—"Open
then the Door!
You know how little while
we have to stay,
And once departed, may
return no more."

IV

ow the New Year reviving
old Desires,
The   thoughtful   Soul   to
Solitude retires,
Where the WHITE HAND
OF MOSES on the Bough
Puts out, and Jesus from the
Ground suspires.

V

Irám indeed is gone with all
    its Rose,
And Jamshýd's Sev'n-ring'd
    Cup where no one
    knows;
    But still the Vine her
    ancient Ruby yields,
And still a Garden by the
    Water blows.

VI

And David's Lips are lock't; but in divine
High - piping Péhlevi, with "Wine! Wine! Wine!
Red Wine!"—the Night-ingale cries to the Rose
That yellow Cheek of hers t' incarnadine.

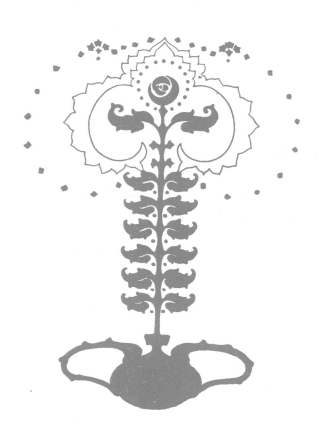

VII

ome, fill the Cup, and in the
Fire of Spring
The Winter Garment of
Repentance fling:
The Bird of Time has but
a little way
To fly—and Lo! the Bird is
on the Wing.

VIII

And look—a thousand Blossoms with the Day
Woke—and a thousand scatter'd into Clay:
    And this first Summer Month that brings the Rose
Shall take Jamshýd and Kaikobád away.

IX

ut come with old Khayyám
and leave the Lot
Of Kaikobád and Kaikhosrú
forgot:
Let Rustum lay about him
as he will,
Or Hátim Tai cry Supper —
heed them not.

X

With me along some Strip of
Herbage strown
That just divides the desert
from the sown,
Where name of Slave and
Sultán scarce is known,
And pity Sultán Máhmúd on
his Throne.

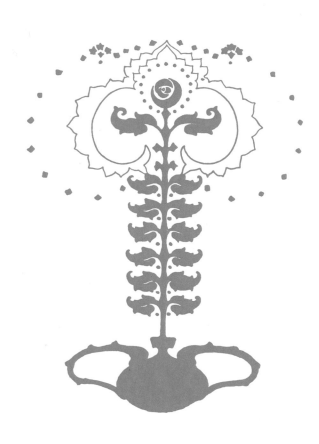

XI

Here with a Loaf of Bread
beneath the Bough,
A Flask of Wine, a Book of
Verse—and Thou
Beside me singing in the
Wilderness—
And Wilderness is Paradise
enow.

XII

"How sweet is mortal Sov-
    ranty!"—think some :
Others — "How blest the
    Paradise to come!"
    Ah, take the Cash in hand
    and waive the Rest ;
Oh, the brave Music of a
    distant Drum !

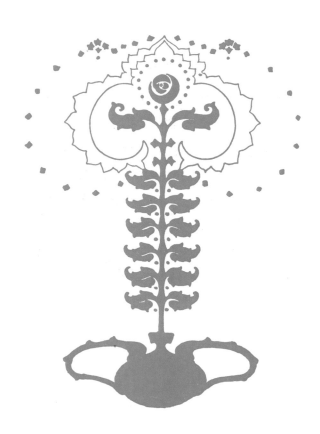

XIII

ook to the Rose that blows
about us—"Lo,
Laughing," she says, "into
the World I blow:
At once the silken Tassel
of my Purse
Tear, and its Treasure on the
Garden throw."

XIV

The Worldly Hope men set
their Hearts upon
Turns Ashes—or it prospers;
and anon,
Like Snow upon the
Desert's dusty Face
Lighting a little Hour or
two—is gone.

XV

And those who husbanded the
   Golden Grain,
And those who flung it to
   the Winds like Rain,
   Alike to no such aureate
   Earth are turn'd
As, buried once, Men want
   dug up again.

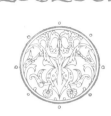

XVI

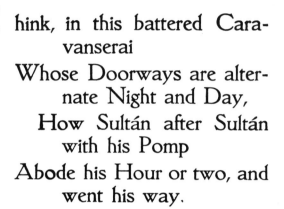

Think, in this battered Cara-
vanserai
Whose Doorways are alter-
nate Night and Day,
How Sultán after Sultán
with his Pomp
Abode his Hour or two, and
went his way.

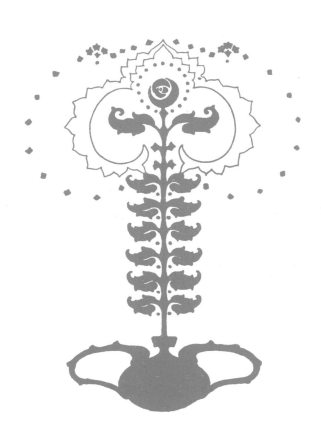

XVII

They say the Lion and the
    Lizard keep
The Courts where Jamshýd
    gloried and drank deep:
And Bahrám, that great
    Hunter—the Wild Ass
Stamps o'er his Head, and he
    lies fast asleep.

XVIII

I sometimes think that never blows so red
   The Rose as where some buried Cæsar bled
   That every Hyacinth the Garden wears
Dropt in its Lap from some once lovely Head.

XIX

nd this delightful Herb whose
tender Green
Fledges the River's Lip on
which we lean—
Ah, lean upon it lightly! for who knows
From what once Lovely Lip
it springs unseen!

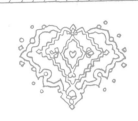

XX

Ah, my Belovéd, fill the cup
that clears
To-day of past Regrets and
future Fears—
To-morrow?— Why, To-
morrow I may be
Myself with Yesterday's
Sev'n Thousand Years.

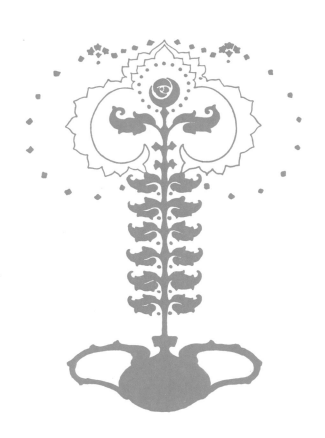

XXI

Lo! some we loved, the love-
liest and the best
That Time and Fate of all
their Vintage prest,
Have drunk their Cup a
Round or two before,
And one by one crept silently
to Rest.

XXII

And we, that now make merry
in the Room
They left, and Summer dresses
in new Bloom,
Ourselves must we beneath
the Couch of Earth
Descend, ourselves to make
a Couch—for whom?

XXIII

Ah, make the most of what we
yet may spend,
Before we too into the Dust
descend;
Dust into Dust, and under
Dust, to lie,
Sans Wine, sans Song, sans
Singer, and—sans End!

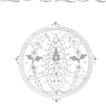

XXIV

like for those who for TO-DAY
    prepare,
And those that after a TO-
    MORROW stare,
A Muezzín from the Tower
    of Darkness cries,
"Fools! your Reward is
    neither Here nor There!"

XXV

hy, all the Saints and Sages
    who discuss'd
Of the Two Worlds so
    learnedly, are thrust
    Like foolish Prophets forth; their Words to Scorn
Are scatter'd, and their
    Mouths are stopt with
    Dust.

XXVI

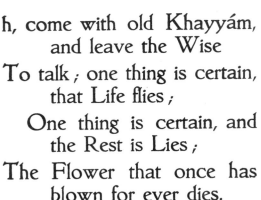

Oh, come with old Khayyám,
and leave the Wise
To talk; one thing is certain,
that Life flies;
One thing is certain, and
the Rest is Lies;
The Flower that once has
blown for ever dies.

XXVII

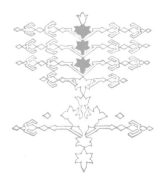

yself when young did eagerly
frequent
Doctor and Saint, and heard
great Argument
About it and about, but
evermore
Came out by the same Door
as in I went.

XXVIII

With them the Seed of Wisdom
did I sow,
And with my own hand
labour'd it to grow:
And this was all the
Harvest that I reap'd—
"I came like Water, and like
Wind I go."

XXIX

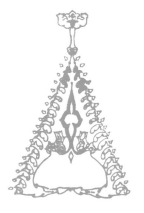

Into this Universe, and *why*
    not knowing,
Nor *whence,* like Water
    willy-nilly flowing!
    And out of it, as Wind
    along the Waste,
I know not *whither,* willy-
    nilly blowing.

XXX

What, without asking, hither
hurried *whence?*
And, without asking, *whither*
hurried hence!
Another and another Cup
to drown
The memory of this Imperti-
nence!

XXXI

p from Earth's Centre through
the Seventh Gate

I rose, and on the Throne of
Saturn sate,

And many Knots unravel'd
by the Road;

But not the Knot of Human
Death and Fate.

XXXII

There was a Door to which I
found no Key:
There was a Veil past which
I could not see:
Some little Talk awhile of
ME and THEE
There seemed—and then no
more of THEE and ME.

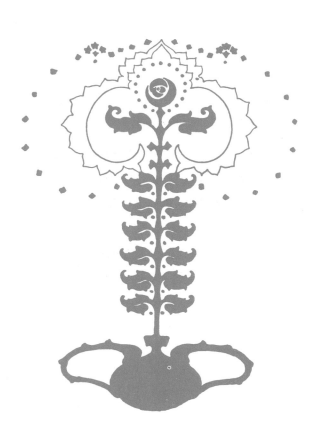

XXXIII

Then to the rolling Heav'n
    itself I cried,
Asking, "What Lamp had
    Destiny to guide
    Her little Children stumbling
    in the Dark?"
And—"A blind understand-
    ing!" Heaven replied.

XXXIV

Then to the earthen Bowl did
    I adjourn
My Lip the secret Well of
    Life to learn:
    And Lip to Lip it murmur'd
    —"While you live
Drink!—for once dead you
    never shall return."

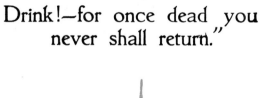

XXXV

I think the Vessel, that with fugitive
Articulation answer'd, once did live,
  And merry-make; and the cold Lip I kiss'd
How many Kisses might it take—and give!

XXXVI

or in the Market-place, one
Dusk of day,
I watch'd the Potter thumping
his wet Clay:
And with its all obliterated
Tongue
It murmur'd — "Gently,
Brother, gently, pray!"

XXXVII

Ah, fill the Cup :—what boots
  it to repeat
How time is slipping under-
  neath our Feet :
  Unborn TO-MORROW and
  dead YESTERDAY,
Why fret about them if
  TO-DAY be sweet!

XXXVIII

ne Moment in Annihilation's
    Waste,
One Moment, of the Well
    of Life to taste—
The Stars are setting and
    the Caravan
Starts for the Dawn of
    Nothing — Oh, make
    haste!

XXXIX

How long, how long, in infinite
  Pursuit
Of This and That endeavour
  and dispute?
    Better be merry with the
    fruitful Grape
Than sadden after none, or
  bitter, Fruit.

XL

You know, my Friends, how
    long since in my House
For a new Marriage I did
    make Carouse:
Divorced   old   barren
    Reason from my Bed,
And took the Daughter of
    the Vine to Spouse.

XLI

or "Is" and "Is-not" though
    with Rule and Line,
And "Up-and-down" *with-
    out,* I could define,
    I yet in all I only cared to
      know,
Was never deep in **anything**
    but—Wine.

XLII

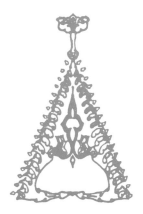

And lately, by the Tavern
    Door agape,
Came stealing through the
    Dusk an Angel Shape
Bearing a Vessel on his
    Shoulder; and
He bid me taste of it; and
    'twas—the Grape!

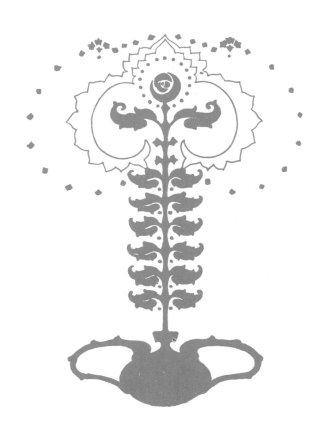

XLIII

The Grape that can with Logic
absolute
The Two-and-Seventy jarring
Sects confute :
The subtle Alchemist that
in a Trice
Life's leaden Metal into Gold
transmute.

XLIV

The mighty Mahmúd, the vic-
torious Lord
That all the misbelieving and
black Horde
Of Fears and Sorrows
that infest the Soul
Scatters and slays with his
enchanted Sword.

XLV

ut leave the Wise to wrangle,
and with me

The Quarrel of the Universe
let be :

And, in some corner of the
Hubbub coucht,

Make Game of that which
makes as much of Thee.

XLVI

For in and out, above, about, below,
'Tis nothing but a Magic Shadow-show,
Play'd in a Box whose Candle is the Sun,
Round which we Phantom Figures come and go.

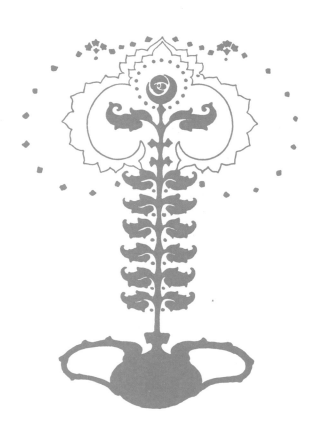

XLVII

And if the Wine you drink, the
Lip you press,
End in the Nothing all Things
end in—Yes—
Then fancy while Thou
art, Thou art but what
Thou shalt be — Nothing —
Thou shalt not be less.

XLVIII

While the Rose blows along the
    River Brink,
With old Khayyám the Ruby
    Vintage drink:
And when the Angel with
    his darker Draught
Draws up to Thee—take that,
    and do not shrink.

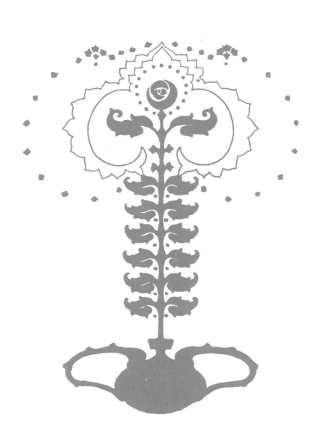

XLIX

'Tis all a Chequer-board of
    Nights and Days
Where Destiny with Men
    for Pieces plays:
    Hither and thither moves,
      and mates, and slays,
And one by one back in the
    Closet lays.

L

he Ball no Question makes
    of Ayes and Noes,
But Right or Left as strikes
    the Player goes;
    And He that toss'd Thee
    down into the Field,
He knows about it all—He
    knows—HE knows!

LI

The Moving Finger writes:
    and, having writ,
Moves on: nor all thy Piety
    nor Wit
    Shall lure it back to cancel
    half a Line,
Nor all thy Tears wash out
    a Word of it.

LII

And that inverted Bowl we call
The Sky,
Whereunder crawling coop't
we live and die,
Lift not thy hands to *It* for
help—for It
Rolls impotently on as Thou
or I.

LIII

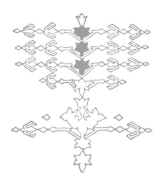

ith Earth's first Clay They
did the last Man's knead,
And then of the Last
Harvest sow'd the Seed:
Yea, the first Morning of
Creation wrote
What the Last Dawn of
Reckoning shall read.

LIV

I tell Thee this—When, starting
from the Goal,
Over the shoulders of the
flaming Foal
Of Heav'n Parwin and
Mushtara they flung,
In my predestin'd Plot of
Dust and Soul

LV

The Vine had struck a Fibre; which about
   If clings my Being—let the Súfi flout;
      Of my Base Metal may be filed a Key,
That shall unlock the Door he howls without.

LVI

And this I know: whether the
    one True Light,
Kindle to Love, or Wrath
    consume me quite,
One Glimpse of It within
    the Tavern caught
Better than in the Temple
    lost outright.

LVII

Oh Thou, who didst with
    Pitfall and with Gin
Beset the Road I was to
    wander in,
    Thou wilt not with Pre-
    destination round
Enmesh me, and impute **my**
    Fall to Sin?

LVIII

Oh Thou, who Man of baser
    Earth didst make
And who with Eden didst
    devise the Snake ;
  For all the Sin wherewith
    the Face of man
Is blacken'd, Man's Forgive-
    ness give—and take !

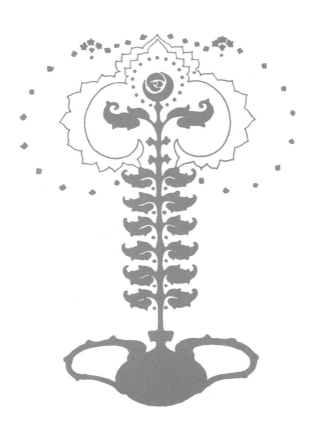

LIX

Listen again. One Evening at the Close
   Of Ramazán, ere the better Moon arose,
   In that old Potter's Shop I stood alone
   With the clay Population round in Rows.

LX

And, strange to tell, among that
    Earthen Lot
Some could articulate, while
    others not :
And suddenly one more
    impatient cried—
"Who *is* the Potter, pray, and
    who the Pot?"

LXI

hen said another—"Surely not
    in vain
"My substance from the com-
    mon Earth was ta'en;
That He who subtly
    wrought me into Shape
Should stamp me back to
    common Earth again."

LXII

Another said—"Why, ne'er a
    peevish Boy
Would break the Bowl from
    which he drank in Joy;
Shall He that *made* the
    Vessel in pure Love
And Fancy, in an after Rage
    destroy!"

LXIII

None answered this; but after
Silence spake
A Vessel of a more ungainly
Make:
"They sneer at me for
leaning all awry;
What! did the Hand then of
the Potter shake?"

LXIV

Said one—"Folks of a surly
   Tapster tell,
And daub his visage with the
   Smoke of Hell;
   They talk of some strict
   Testing of us—Pish!
He's a Good Fellow and
   'twill all be well."

LXV

hen said another with a long-
  drawn Sigh,
"My Clay with long Oblivion
  is gone dry :
But, fill me with the old
  familiar Juice,
Methinks I might recover by-
  and-bye!"

LXVI

So while the Vessels one by
one were speaking,
One spied the little Crescent
all were seeking:
And then they jogged each
other, "Brother! Brother!
Hark to the Porter's Shoulder-
knot a-creaking!"

LXVII

Ah, with the Grape my fading
Life provide,
And wash my Body whence
the Life has died,
And in a Winding-sheet
of Vine-leaf wrapt,
So bury me by some sweet
Garden side.

LXVIII

hat ev'n my buried Ashes such a Snare
Of Perfume shall fling up into the Air,
    As not a True Believer passing by
But shall be overtaken un-aware.

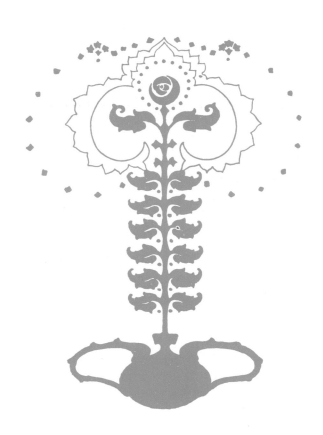

LXIX

Indeed the Idols I have loved
    so long
Have done my Credit in
    Men's Eye much Wrong,
Have drowned my Honour
    in a shallow Cup,
And sold my Reputation for
    a Song.

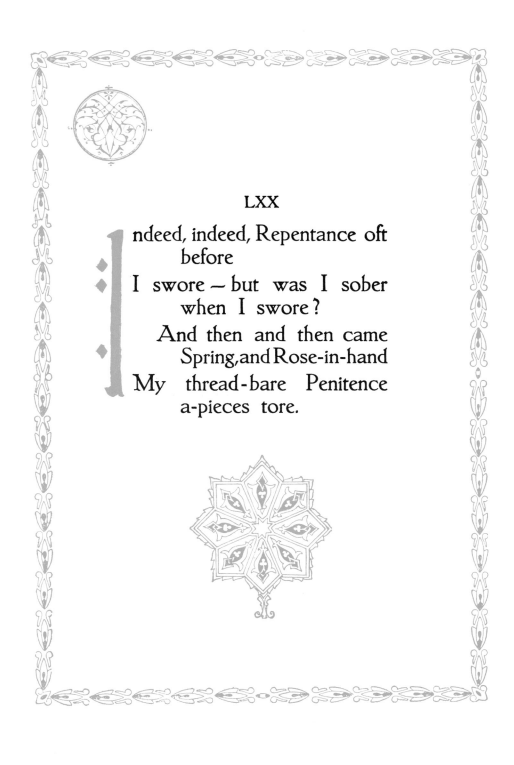

LXX

Indeed, indeed, Repentance oft
   before
I swore — but was I sober
   when I swore?
And then and then came
   Spring, and Rose-in-hand
My thread-bare Penitence
   a-pieces tore.

LXXI

And much as Wine has played
　　the Infidel,
And robb'd me of my Robe
　　of Honour—well,
　I often wonder what the
　　Vintners buy
One half so precious as the
　　Goods they sell.

LXXII

las, that Spring should vanish
    with the Rose!
That Youth's sweet-scented
    Manuscript should close!
The Nightingale that in the
    Branches sang,
Ah, whence, and whither flown
    again, who knows?

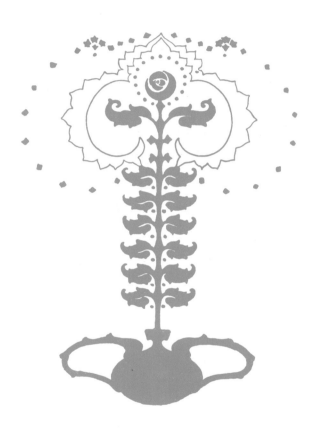

LXXIII

Ah, Love! could thou and I
    with Fate conspire
To grasp this sorry Scheme
    of Things entire,
    Would not we shatter it
    to bits and then
Re-mould it nearer to the
    Heart's Desire!

LXXIV

A h, Moon of my Delight who
    know'st no Wane,
The Moon of Heaven is
    rising once again:
   How oft hereafter rising
    shall she look
Through this same Garden
    after me—in vain!

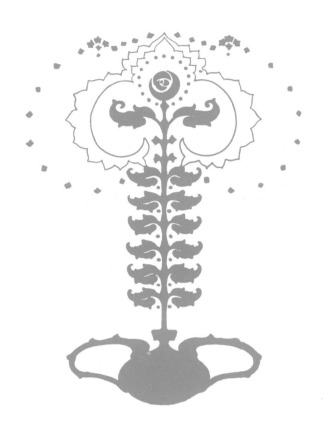